CCJc
8/09

D1498015

Short Vowel Phonics 2:
short a, i

by: Patricia J. Norton

illustrated by: Sarah E. Cashman

Other reading material by the Author:

Short Vowel Phonics 1
Short Vowel Phonics 2, short o, u, e
Short Vowel Phonics 3
Short Vowel Phonics 4
Short Vowel Phonics Short Stories
Decodable Alphabet Chart

The short "a" stories are dedicated to all parents
and teachers of struggling readers.

The story "The Twin Swim" is dedicated to my neighbors,
Debbie and Richard, whose "big tin" swimming pool
inspired the story.

ISBN: 978-0-9817710-1-4 (lib. bdg.)
[1. Reading - Phonetic method. 2. Reading readiness. 3. Phonics]

shortvowelphonics.com

Manufactured in the United States of America

Text font: Pen Time Manuscript

Tc

Short a Stories

Short i Stories

Ram the Rat

Note to parents and teachers: Please have the child read the title before beginning the story. The title of the story, the pictures and the text are coordinated in such a way that a child will have read the word once before they are shown a picture of the word. This is to insure the child is learning to decode the word and not just guess.

Ram is a rat.

The rat sat.

Dad has a ham.

Dad has a yam.

Ram ran.

Ram can nab the ham.

Dad had a ham.

Dad is a tad mad.

Max the Cat

Max is a cat.

Max can nap and nap

and nap.

Jan has a fan.

Can Jan fan the cat?

Sam is a lad.

Can Sam pat the cat?

Max ran and ran.

Max had a nap.

Jan can fan the cat.

Sam can pat the cat.

The Last Lap

Pam is Fran's pal.

Pam and Fran ran.

Fran ran a lap.

Pam ran a lap.

Pam ran fast.

Pam ran past Fran.

Pant! Pant! Fran is last.

Is Pam Fran's pal?

Brad the Lad

Brad is a lad.

Brad swam.

Brad has a bad cramp.

Brad is sad.

Brad can grab the raft.

Brad had a nap at the raft.

Brad is glad.

Brad swam at the land.

Land has sand.

Land is grand!

Ask Brad.

The Big Rig

Liz is a kid.

Liz is Vic's kin.

Liz hid in Vic's big rig.

Liz has a wig.

The wig did rip in the rig.

Vic did fix the wig.

Dig, Dig, Dig

Jin is a big kid.

Jin did dig.

Jin did dig and dig.

Jin did dig a pit.

Jin hit a big tin in the pit.

Jin did a jig.

In the tin is a pin.

Did Jin hit it big?

The Twin Swim

Jim is a twin.

And Sid is a twin.

Sid is Jim's twin.

Sid and Jim swim.

Sid and Jim swim in a big,

big tin.

Sid did twist and spin.

Sid hit the tin rim.

Sid is grim.

Jim did a dip and a flip.

Jim did slip and hit his hip.

Jim is grim.

Jim and Sid quit the swim

in the big tin.

Jim and Sid sit and drip.